W9-BNQ-995

AZUSA STREET
TILL NOW

CLARA DAVIS

w Whitaker House

All Scripture quotations are taken from the *King James Version* (KJV) of the Bible.

AZUSA STREET TILL NOW

ISBN: 0-88368-272-9
Printed in the United States of America
Copyright© 1993 by Whitaker House

Whitaker House
580 Pittsburgh Street
Springdale, PA 15144

Contents

Foreword

Clara Davis is a prime example of a Christian mother, pastor's wife, and ordained minister of the Gospel. She was preaching revival meetings before she met R. L. Davis, her husband. Together they built six churches and ministered all over the United States and Canada. She has also been president of the Odessa, Texas, chapter of Women's Aglow.

Clara is mother of three sons who are all in full-time ministry.

Her prayer life is surely the key to her success.

In this book you will read through the history of a family from covered-wagon days through the Azusa Street outpouring of the Holy Spirit and soap-box preaching and into these modern days. The book is destined to be a classic.

I am proud of my mother.

Burnie Davis

Introduction

The purpose of this book, in the mind of the author, is to show the move of the Holy Spirit in this twentieth century.

In the past, the church of Jesus Christ has gone through various stages of highs and lows. At certain times, mighty revivals have come, ushering in some of the great denominations of our day. At other times, the church has experienced a falling away and general lethargy.

We must have another great outpouring of the Holy Spirit in our day, now. Acts 2:17 states, *"It shall come to pass in the last days, saith God, I will pour out my spirit upon all flesh."* Jesus told His disciples, *"But ye shall receive power; after that the Holy Ghost is come upon you: and ye shall be witnesses unto me...unto the uttermost part of the earth"* (Acts 1:8).

Without the power of the Holy Spirit of God, the church stands helpless to accomplish the great task of getting the Gospel out to the ends of the world.

> [1]*Blow ye the trumpet in zion, and sound an alarm in my holy mountain: let all the inhabitants of the land tremble: for the day of the Lord cometh, for it is nigh at hand.*　　　　　　*(Joel 2:1)*

Can we hear the clarion call? God is calling His people like a mighty army to arise, united in the power of the Spirit to go forth and perform the works of Christ.

Jesus told His disciples, *"Verily, verily, I say unto you, He that believeth on me, the works that I do shall he do also; and greater works than these shall he do; because I go unto my father"* (John 14:12).

1

The Twentieth-Century Awakening

Traveling down a dusty road in West Texas in a wagon drawn by a fine team of horses was a young couple and their two little boys. This family of Texans had gathered together their meager belongings and had set out for California. It was the year 1895. These were my parents and my two older brothers.

Dad had evidently heard the call: "Go west, young man." His sisters and brothers were already living in California, and he thought perhaps he could find a better life for his family there, too.

Dad was an old cowhand who had ridden the range for years. He had herded cattle through many a dangerous situation. But could he bear to leave these beautiful animals behind? "Yes!" He would just hook up the team to the wagon and drive out to California. They could make it, somehow.

This hardy little band of pioneers had not gone very far when a terrible storm came up. The sky turned black as thunder and lightning began to lash out their warnings that it was time to run for shelter. The family stopped at a nearby farmhouse just in time: the bottom seemed to fall out of the sky in what was called in those days a "waterspout." This simple churchgoing family was shocked as they listened while the farmer shook his fist at God and cursed Him for allowing his crop to be destroyed by the storm.

When the storm had subsided, my parents realized that they were no match for the elements, much less for this long and hazardous journey that lay ahead of them. Dad decided to sell his horses and wagon and buy train tickets to California.

When they arrived in California, they finally settled in the town of Downey, which was a suburb of Los Angeles. Things were quite different then from what they are now. Los Angeles was an overgrown town filled with horses and buggies. My father got a job hauling brick with a team of horses through the main part of the city.

My parents and brothers were a young family, used to the wide open spaces and freedom of the range. They were now beginning a new way of life in the hustle and bustle of the city. They were a God-fearing family, having been raised in the Methodist church. However, they had not as yet had a born-again experience of salvation. They felt a need of the boys being in church, so they began attending a Holiness church which at that time was much like the Methodist church. They would later tell of great revivals in those days in which the power of God would fall and people would lay under that power for hours. They called it being in a trance.

It was during this time that another son was added to the family. They named him Winfred Lloyd. The older boys were called Henry and Earl.

This particular Holiness group which the family joined was made up of about twenty churches in the Los Angeles area. They gathered together once a year for a great camp meeting. Their heart cry was always the same: "Lord, send us a revival."

Mother said that she thought she was saved until conviction came to her one night in one of those meetings. "I realized I had not been born again," she said, "but was trying to live a good moral life.

14

Salvation is such a wonderful experience! How good it is to know one is truly a child of God and ready to meet the Lord when He comes."

It was while they were living in Downey, California, that my father became acquainted with Brother W. J. Seymour. Brother Seymour was alive and afire with the great news of a magnificent spiritual revival that was going on in Houston and Kansas City. There people were encountering the same infilling of the Spirit as the disciples had experienced on the day of Pentecost as recorded in the second chapter of Acts.

Brother Seymour was speaking at the time in a black Holiness church not far from where my folks lived. Dad liked to go to the meetings on Sunday afternoons. Dad was deeply impressed with the message that Brother Seymour was bringing, as his heart was crying out to God for a deeper walk with Him. "Yes," Dad reported to the family, "people were actually speaking in other tongues as the Spirit gave utterance." This was new to the family since they had always believed that a person was filled with the Holy Ghost at the moment of sanctification. Yet, it was obvious that these people had received a special anointing of the Spirit of God.

It is truly the operation of the Holy Spirit by which a person is converted and born into the family of God. We are born of the Spirit, led by the Spirit, baptized with the Spirit. We are commanded to be *"filled with the spirit"* (Ephesians 5:18).

It has been hard for the church world to understand the full potential of a truly Spirit-filled life. Christ told His disciples in Acts 1:8, *"Ye shall receive power, after that the Holy Ghost is come upon you; and ye shall be witnesses unto me...unto the uttermost part of the earth."*

Although the early church had started out with this empowerment and had seen miracles of healing and casting out of demons, somehow through the ages, the church had lost that original vitality. Now, realizing their lack, many Christians were beginning to cry out to God for a renewal of this power. But the church world in general, not seeing the might of God manifested in their day as it was in the beginning, had convinced themselves that this power was just for the early church. They argued that the first disciples needed this gifting to help get the church started, but felt that God no longer moved in that manner.

The question is, if the early church needed this power to become established on earth, why then is that same power supposedly denied the present-day church which is preparing for the second coming of the Lord Jesus Christ? Is this experience truly for our day? If not, why not? Jesus said in the Sermon on the Mount, *"Blessed are they which do hunger and thirst after righteousness: for they shall be filled"* (Matthew 5:6). Where there is a hunger and desire to be filled with righteousness, the Lord is ready and willing to meet that desire.

My family was there to witness and to participate in the greatest revival that was to shake the world since the day of Pentecost. The outpouring of the Holy Spirit had come to Topeka, Kansas, in 1901 in a Bible school. Then it broke out in Houston, Texas, and spread to Los Angeles, California. From there, the fire of God was being manifested around the world. This was in the year 1906.

2

The Comforter Has Come

In the city of Topeka, Kansas, in 1901, the Reverend Charles F. Parham and his Bible students from Bethel College, which consisted of forty students, were studying the book of Acts. Just before Christmas, Rev. Parham left for a three-day preaching mission. Before going, he asked his students to determine what would be considered the New Testament evidence of the baptism of the Holy Spirit.

He told them that there was a great interest in this subject in various parts of the country. Some claimed this experience by faith, without any special evidence, while others considered joyous demonstrations such as shouting or jumping as the evidence. Many thought it was a special anointing or sanctification.

"But," said Brother Parham, "Though I honor the Spirit in all of these manifestations and graces, yet I believe there is a greater manifestation and power. Now, students," he counseled, "while I am gone, see if there is not some evidence given of the baptism of the Holy Spirit, so there can be no doubt on the subject."

When he returned, Brother Parham called the students together and asked them what they had discovered. They all gave the same report. They said that there were different things which occurred when the Pentecostal blessings fell, but the one indisputable proof on each occasion was that those who had received the Spirit had spoken with other tongues.

While there had been recorded many instances of persons speaking in tongues before the year 1900, in each case, the "speaking in tongues" was considered a special phenomenon, or, at the most, a gift of the Spirit, with the result that no special emphasis had been made which would cause those who were seeking the fullness of the Spirit to expect to speak in tongues. But these students believed that speaking in tongues was the initial evidence of a person's having received the baptism of the Holy Ghost.

These students began to pray that they might have this experience, as evidenced in the second, tenth, and nineteenth chapters of the book of Acts. One of these students, Agnes Ozman, gives this account:

"On watch night, we had a blessed service, praying that God's blessing might rest upon us as the new year came in. During the first day of 1901, the presence of the

Lord was with us in a marked way, stilling hearts to wait upon Him for greater things. The spirit of prayer was upon us in the evening. It was nearly 11 o'clock on this first of January when it came into my heart to ask that hands might be laid upon me that I might receive the gift of the Holy Ghost.

"As hands were laid upon my head, the Holy Spirit fell on me, and I began to speak in tongues, glorifying God...I had the added joy that my heart longed for, and a depth of the presence of the Lord within that I never knew before. It was as if rivers of living water were proceeding from my innermost being.

"I was the first to speak in tongues in the Bible school, and it seemed to me that the rest were wanting to talk in tongues, too. But I told them not to seek for tongues, but to seek for the Holy Ghost...

"It was some months later that I was fully persuaded in my own heart about the evidence of the baptism...I watched nine different ones receive the Holy Spirit, saying to myself and before God, 'I will see if everyone talks in tongues,' and one by one everyone received the Holy Spirit and began to speak in other tongues as the Spirit gave them utterance."

Parham himself received this Pentecostal baptism on January 3, 1901.[1] The news of these happenings quickly spread. This love of God began to extend to Missouri and Texas. Many people were being filled with this wonderful presence of the Holy Ghost.

I should like to add here that while I believe that speaking in tongues is the initial physical evidence of the Holy Ghost

---

[1]"Pentecostal Revival Now 75 Years Old," *The Pentecostal Evangel* (January 4, 1976).

baptism, the real purpose of the coming of the Holy Spirit is that one be enpowered from on high. (See Acts 1:8.) Speaking in tongues is given as a sign and as a means of worship and personal edification. It is a prayer language, given for intercession in prayer. It is also given as a means of prophetic utterance when followed by the gift of interpretation to benefit the church.

The revival soon spread to Azusa Street in Los Angeles, California. My oldest brother, Henry McGowan, was privileged to attend these meetings with our parents and very vividly recalls those days. He was fourteen years old at the time of this great outpouring in Los Angeles. The following is an eyewitness account he recorded for me:

I am writing what I personally saw of the outpouring of the Holy Spirit in the Azusa Street Mission. Azusa Street is just one block long, near where Los Angeles and Main Streets merge.

The Comforter Has Come

Years ago the Methodists built a church there. It was a two-story structure made entirely of wood, with the upstairs used as Sunday school rooms. Later, larger warehouses began to build all around them. The Methodists decided to sell and build elsewhere. It was now being used as a warehouse and stable for hay and stock.

Brother W. J. Seymour, a black brother from Houston, Texas, had found this place and had opened it up for services. My family were members of what they called the Holiness church. The Free Methodist church and the Holiness church were almost identical in doctrine. This was a small organization of just twenty-six churches, mostly in the Los Angeles area.

There was a black Holiness church near where our family lived. It was pastored by a woman by the name of Sister Hutchinson. It was she who invited Brother Seymour to her church for a meeting. He had just come from a great revival in Houston, Texas, where God was filling people with the Holy Ghost, and they were speaking in other tongues. He had not received this experience as yet, but believed in his heart that this was for today. He was preaching this in the church.

My father, W. H. McGowan, would slip out to the meetings to hear him without telling the rest of his family. It sounded like what my father was looking for. After hearing him several times, my father was convinced it was real.

Our church had a camp meeting every year in the month of August, near Downey, which we always attended. In 1905, the preachers were proclaiming that God wanted to send an outpouring of the Holy Ghost upon His people, and if our church did not dig in and get what God had for us, He would raise up a people who would. These people were hungry for God, but felt that it had to come by their little book of rules.

Since my father had become interested in what was going on in Sister Hutchison's church, he felt that the General Superintendent should know about it. He sent for him to come hear Brother Seymour. After the Superintendent had heard him, he got up and said that he was glad Brother Seymour wanted the baptism of the Holy Ghost and that he hoped he would soon receive it. However, he said that our church already had this experience. (They felt that when they were sanctified, they were filled with the Holy Spirit, but they did not believe that speaking in tongues was for our day.)

After the service, the Superintendent went to Brother Seymour and asked him not to preach this anymore in that church. He could speak with authority since all the churches were linked with the General Assembly.

When the people found out what had happened, Brother Seymour was invited to one of their homes on Bonnie Bray Street. This was a middle-class section with nice homes, but not wealthy. That night the fire of God fell, and a few people were filled with the Holy Ghost according to Acts 2:4. Brother Seymour was one of them. The next night the place was packed out.

He was shown an old, abandoned building that had been used as a church but now was a warehouse. They cleaned the place out, made makeshift benches, and used an old dry-goods box for a pulpit. He didn't do much preaching after it got going, but spent most of his time behind this old box with his head in it praying.

He used the old Sunday school rooms upstairs to live in. News of what was going on soon spread all over the world like a prairie fire. People were hungry for God. Special prayer meetings were going on everywhere. God had put a new hope in people's hearts. They would meet early in the morning and start singing. They had no song book and no piano, but, oh, what singing! One of their main songs was "The Comforter Has Come."

For a long time people had been crying out for a deeper walk with God. Now it had come, and people were so excited about it. They would sing for a while, and then those who had been filled with the Holy Ghost would get up and tell about it and how wonderful it was. After some testimonies, someone would preach and tell what God had promised. Then it would start all over again, going on almost all night. If anyone was hungry, they would leave for something to eat and then return as soon as possible.

Dad was hauling brick with a team of mules at this time. He would stop and listen and forget to go back to work; he was so lost in the Lord and what was going on.

My father got up in his Holiness church one day and said that he was convinced that he had found what he was hungry for. He felt that if they fought against this love of God as individuals or as a church, that they would die spiritually.

The pastor had not heard about it, but he said, "This may be our answer to our hunger for God. How many will meet me here tomorrow for an all-day prayer meeting and inquire of God what He has to say about this?" Most of the number came. Before the day was over, God had filled a woman with the Holy Ghost. From then on, we started going to Azusa Street every night except our service night.

The Comforter Has Come

Mother received the Holy Spirit before April of that year. It was camp meeting time for our churches in Downey. We had always attended. We were like a big family. Mother felt God wanted her to give her testimony to show them that this was what God wanted them to have.

Mother prayed almost continually. While she was washing dishes, she had her Bible open, she would stop and read awhile, and go on crying and praying.

When camp meeting came, she could hardly wait to tell how wonderfully God was blessing her. She sat down broken-hearted as they rejected her message.

***

But we will let Mother tell her own story.

3

Another Echo from Azusa

The following is Mother McGowan's testimony of Azusa Street which has been condensed from a tract entitled *Another Echo From Azusa,* which she wrote at the age of 84:

The Holy Spirit moved in my life in such a mighty way in 1906, during the great outpouring of the Holy Spirit as it came to Los Angeles, California. My family and I were at this time members of the Holiness church. They were a wonderful, clean people, desirous of the moving of God's Spirit. However, when the Holy

Spirit came in a manner in which they did not expect and people began speaking in other tongues as in the Book of Acts, they would not accept it as being from God. The majority of professing Christian leaders rejected it as heresy. The power of God always brings conflict and struggle when He moves among Christian people.

When my husband and I came to Downey, California, in July, 1895, we were Methodists. However, I was not born again. I thought I was, as this is the way I had been taught. It was not long until I got saved. One night there were five different people who came and tried to get me to go to the altar, but I couldn't move; I seemed bound to my chair. All at once the Lord spoke to me, "Are you going to disobey Me?" I said, "No!" and went to the altar and was wonderfully saved.

I shall never forget the preacher's text that night: *"Zacchaeus, come down, for this*

34

day I must dine with thee" (Luke 19:5). I
went to the altar, for every word was for
me. The preacher came to me and asked,
"Aren't you saved? Get up and tell it." I
did, and the fire of God came down in my
soul from the tips of my fingers to the ends
of my toes. I felt like Isaiah saying, "A live
coal touched my lips." (See Isaiah 6:6-7.)
He certainly did save and sanctify me; not
only that, but He healed my body, too. I
was having inward fever every day. I was
nothing but skin and bones. From that
time on I began to get better.

I have always believed that had I had
the light on the baptism of the Holy Ghost
according to Acts 2:4, I would have been
filled that night. But I had to wait until
the power fell in Los Angeles.

When Brother Seymour came to Los
Angeles to preach in this little Holiness
church at the pastor's invitation, he began
to preach what he had seen in Houston,

Texas. He had seen people being filled with the Holy Ghost and speaking in tongues. His message was not accepted by the pastor and the superintendent. He was asked to discontinue preaching this doctrine. From there he went to a home on Bonnie Bray Street and then to this building on Azusa Street.

As soon as my husband heard about it, he was anxious to go. However, he said, "They are saying we do not have the Holy Ghost." This put unbelief in my heart. We Holiness people believed we received the Holy Ghost when we were sanctified. Actually, no one can be saved or sanctified without the operation of the Holy Ghost; but we were to find out later that we did not have the fullness of the power of the Holy Spirit as they had received it on the Day of Pentecost.

We went one night to the meeting, and it nearly scared me to death when we heard them speak with tongues. I thought, if this is the way I feel, I don't want to go back. Mr. McGowan said, "You had better be careful; this is of God." I went back again, and this time it didn't seem so bad. I kept going back, and I am so glad that I did.

One night there were five or six men and women sitting on the platform. All at once they all began singing in the spirit. I sat there spellbound. I thought I had never heard such singing in all my life. As I began to acknowledge in my heart that it sounded like the angels singing, the Lord began to bless my soul. That night all unbelief was gone; after that it was sweet to me. The meetings went on every night with a full house. Sinners would pass the door and come in and get saved.

One afternoon I was listening to the testimonies; they were wonderful. I said to the Lord, "I would love to have what these people have. I don't care if I speak in tongues or not." The Lord said, "I want you to get the Holy Ghost and take it to my people." I said, "Lord, Lord, how can I take it to them? I cannot preach, but I am willing to do anything I can." That was all the Lord wanted, a willing vessel. From that time on, I was very hungry for the Holy Ghost. A few days later I was praying, "Lord, I would like to know You are going to use me." The Lord said, "I am going to manifest Myself through you."

I hardly understood what He meant. I went to the Holiness church that night and seemed unusually happy. I wanted to sing and testify, but I had a cold and couldn't speak above a whisper. However, I was singing and making melody in my heart to the Lord.

When the preacher finished, the Lord picked me up like the wind would a feather and took me around the congregation three times. The fourth time He took me between the pulpit and the altar; there I stood, beckoning with my hands for the people to come to the altar. Our pastor said, "The Lord is calling, 'Come.'" It looked like everyone in the house came forward. Oh, what a meeting we had! The Lord said, "This is the way I am going to use you. I will manifest Myself through you."

A little later I received the baptism of the Holy Ghost. It happened after everyone but five or six people had left. They were asking someone about Pentecost. I was not interested. I sat by the altar with my Bible in my lap, turning the pages, asking the Lord to help me find the answer as to why I had not received this experience. I overheard someone ask why it takes some people so long to receive the Holy Ghost. The preacher said, "The lack of faith." I called to him and asked, "Do you think it is unbelief that I do not receive the Holy Spirit?" He answered, "Yes."

I laid my Bible on the altar and threw up my hands and said, "Lord, I receive." I said that perhaps three times when the power of God fell on me. I lay under the power from midnight until three o'clock in the morning. I then began singing in the Spirit for some time. Oh, how I sang! Then the Spirit took my lips and spoke in tongues. My, but the power did fall! This was indeed the endowment of power.

***

The Lord used Mother in the Holiness services in singing in the Spirit, and manifested Himself in some tremendous ways. Though some did accept, along with their pastor, Brother Pendleton, the conference ruled speaking in tongues off-limits on the campground. Mother continued:

I was grieved in my heart and asked the Lord, "Why is it that God's people will fight one against the other? They are Your people, and I am Yours." This Scripture came to me:

> [7]*Unto you therefore which believe he is precious: but unto them which be disobedient, the stone which the builders disallowed, the same is made the head of the corner,*
> [8]*And a stone of stumbling, and a rock of offense, even to them which stumble at the word, being disobedient: whereunto also they were appointed.*   (1 Peter 2:7-8)

At the camp meeting one day we were told that if we would give up speaking in tongues, we could keep our church. Of course, we would not give up what God had done for us, so by the next Sunday our pastor had rented a place on Eighth and Maple Streets in Los Angeles. Arrangements had been made to take the congregation by streetcar to the new location. That morning the pastor said to the congregation, "All who feel as I do may come and go with me." All but three went to the other building, as they had the lights on and prepared for the occasion.

The pastor asked how many would meet him at the church to pray for God's Spirit on them there. Brother Pendleton said he could not be there that early, so he gave my husband the keys and asked him to open the building. He was there about 5:00 A.M. and found the yard full of people. They said, "I thought you were going to be here early." No wonder God answered prayer and gave revival.

Thus was the first Pentecostal church begun in Los Angeles. The neighbors had followed us to church. They felt that the leaders had turned out God's people.

As the service began, I looked down in my lap and read this Scripture passage:

> *[1]Behold, what manner of love the Father hath bestowed upon us, that we should be*

> *called the sons of God: therefore the world*
> *knoweth us not, because it knew him not.*
> *²Beloved, now are we the sons of God, and*
> *it doth not yet appear what we shall be:*
> *but we know that, when he shall appear,*
> *we shall be like him; for we shall see him*
> *as he is.*   *(1 John 3:1-2)*

I thought I had never felt such love before. When the preacher got through preaching, the Lord picked me up and took me to the front speaking in tongues. There He preached a sermon through me on the above text. The people came running to the altar. We don't always understand the workings of God.

***

Mother never lost the burden for her beloved church. She was so grieved that they did not recognize the move of God when He came. Of course, many of the denominational churches did not recognize it either and rejected it as heresy. Although they were praying for revival and asking God to send His Holy Spirit to move among them, they could not accept the manner in which He came. Has not this been the case down through the generations?

Israel could not accept their Messiah either. They had expected their King to come in a more respectable place than an oxen stable, with a little more class, catering to a higher class of people. But the poor heard Him gladly. (See Mark 12:37.) Any new move of God's Spirit is sometimes rather shocking to the natural mind of man. All things indeed must be judged by the Scriptures.

4

Pentecostal Denominations Form

I n referring back to the outpouring of the Holy Spirit in the early 1900s, we need to know some of the background for the organizing of the different Pentecostal groups which took place at that time.

Those people, such as my folks and many others, who began to experience and share about the baptism of the Holy Spirit soon discovered that they were no longer welcome in their own churches. Many of the leaders of these churches were fine Christian people who loved the Lord, but they were just not prepared for such a spiritual revolution. It rocked their church doctrines and traditions. It was the same way when Christ came to earth: the religious bodies of that day were not prepared for His coming. Consequently, there was nothing left for these Spirit-filled Christians to do but to gather together with those of like precious faith with whom they could worship, forming their own churches.

Missionaries soon came from all over the world to witness this new outpouring of the Holy Spirit. They began to take news of it back to their fields of labor and to share this message with others. Revival seemed to break out spontaneously all over the world. It was God's time to shake the world with revival fires which were to get the church ready for His approaching return.

The fruit and the gifts of the Spirit were in evidence everywhere. However, the manifestations were labeled "emotionalism" and "fanaticism" by many of the older denominational leaders.

Pentecostals would be the first to admit that there have been mistakes and excesses. All who claimed did not possess. Many of those who did possess still had much to overcome, both in lack of wisdom and carnality. It is always easy in times like this for the enemy to take advantage of people's enthusiasm and inexperience by bringing in false doctrine, even as in Paul's day when errors and misconceptions had to be combatted.

However, for these reasons, and also to bring about a unification of biblical doctrine and to meet the need for fellowship of believers drawn together by what was called "their distinctive testimony of speaking in other tongues as the Spirit gave them utterance upon receiving the Holy Spirit," it seemed necessary to establish some kind of church government to protect the work of God and to carry this message to the ends of the world.

So there began to come into existence Pentecostal denominations such as the Assemblies of God, which was organized in Hot Springs, Arkansas, in 1914. There also were the Church of God, the Pentecostal Holiness Church, the Foursquare Church, and others of an independent nature. Where they might have varied in some details, they stood together on the basic doctrines of the Bible such as salvation through the atoning blood of Jesus Christ who was born of a virgin, the Holy Ghost baptism according to Acts 2:4, the second coming of Christ, divine healing, and the gifts of the Spirit.

Because of persecution and misunderstanding, some felt that Pentecostals were appearing to have a "holier than thou" attitude. God forbid! If Pentecostals have anything, it is because of the grace of God and not because of anything of which they themselves can boast.

Standards of holiness have varied in the opinion of many congregations. We all would do well to stick to Bible standards and not be judges in trivial matters. The Scriptures teach us to *"Follow...holiness, without which no man shall see the Lord"* (Hebrews 12:14).

The gifts of the Spirit are of great value to the church and should be in operation in the body of Christ, as recorded in First Corinthians, chapters 12 and 14. However, without the love manifested in the thirteenth chapter, they would be of little value.

Some of the largest and most evangelistic churches in the world today are Pentecostal. The Pentecostal movement has been called by some the "third force" in church leadership. It had its beginnings in meetings out in the open air, in school houses, under brush arbors, and in vacant or abandoned buildings often on the wrong side of the railroad tracks. We have seen these churches grow into beautiful temples in the main areas of the cities.

The foreign missions program of these Pentecostal organizations has been responsible for the establishment and maintenance of many schools, orphanages, and evangelistic centers around the world. The emphasis of this program is to train foreign nationals to be leaders and pastors of their own people. It is the aim of these churches to make foreign missions work indigenous. Should a nation ever close its doors to American missionaries, these nationals will be able to carry on the work on their own without having to depend upon outsiders.

There is no way the world can ignore such a movement. The more it has been fought, the faster it has grown. Today is our day! It is the day for the church of the Lord Jesus Christ to arise and do exploits. It is also a day when false doctrines and false Christs are making great strides in their efforts to sidetrack sincere people into believing a lie and being damned. It is not a day to join the church of Laodicea of the book of Revelation, those who were rich and increased with goods and in need of nothing so that they had become lukewarm and self-satisfied. Christ said of this church that He would spew them out of His mouth. (See Revelation 3:14-18.)

We thank God for all denominations that have begun in the Spirit and have kept Christ as the center. We thank God for the way He has manifested Himself through the Pentecostal denominations and fellowships of our day. Many have a rich heritage handed down to them by the old-line denominations who pioneered the way and who brought God's people to the point of a real hunger for the deeper things of

God. And God is filling many of those people today as they open their hearts to His Spirit.

Donald Gee, a great apostle of the Pentecostals, sounds out a warning in his book, *Now That You Have Been Baptized with the Spirit*: "We must have another Pentecost, and I greatly deplore the narrowing down of the vision of our beloved Pentecostal people. Some of our people are becoming denominational. May God make us bigger."[1]

It makes no difference about our experiences of the past. It is what we have today that counts. There must be a daily renewing. The danger is that we will throw up walls around our own groups so high that hungry hearts who may be looking our way cannot feel free to come in and out and

---

[1]Donald Gee, *Now That You Have Been Baptized with the Spirit* (Springfield, MO: Gospel Publishing House), 63.

find pasture. Spiritual pride and prejudice hinder the free moving of the Holy Spirit.

Another danger for nondenominationals is developing a pride of independence. We are all the body of Christ and need one another. May God give us balance that we might be able to recognize the move of God wherever it is flowing.

In the lands where there is persecution of Christians, denominational ties do not matter. Where the forces of Communism, Mohammedanism, Buddhism, and Satan worship are coming against Christians, we are made to realize that there is one common bond in the person of the Lord Jesus Christ.

When a great flood hits a city, the high and the low all flow together in one common level of destruction. Likewise, when a Holy Ghost revival hits a city, God's Spirit causes the high places and low places to flow together. Those of the highest echelons of society and those of the lowest strata of life soon find a common meeting place in Christ and the power of the Holy Spirit.

A delight for these Pentecostal groups has been to see how God has broken forth in many of our old-line denominations and to watch how they are now being filled with the power of the Holy Spirit. God is moving throughout the earth toward any and all who are hungry for a move of His Spirit, regardless of their denominational affiliation.

5

This Generation

I n the twenty-second chapter of Luke, Jesus gave His disciples several signs of the end of the age and of His return to earth. He concluded His remarks by stating: *"This generation shall not pass away till all be fulfilled"* (v. 32). Of what generation was Jesus speaking? This is an all-important question. What will be the sign of His coming and of the end of the earth?

Many people are confused about this subject. It is obvious that Jesus was not referring to His generation when He spoke of *"this generation,"* because that generation has long since passed on without His return. A more reasonable interpretation of

Jesus' statement would be that Jesus was saying that the generation which sees all these signs coming to pass in their day would not pass away before His appearance in the heavens. In other words, "When you see these signs, know that before your generation has passed, I shall return!"

God, through His Word, spoke to many generations that have come and gone from the time of Adam and Eve. God made a covenant with the generations of men. *"He hath remembered his covenant for ever, the word which he commanded to a thousand generations"* (Psalm 105:8).

There will be one generation which will be on the earth when Christ returns, even as there was one particular generation which witnessed the first coming of Christ to the earth. They witnessed His birth, His ministry and miracles, His death and resurrection, and His return to heaven. They witnessed the angel who gave the promise that *"this same Jesus, which is taken up from you into heaven, shall so come in like manner as ye have seen him go into heaven"* (Acts 1:11).

There will be one generation who will cry with the apostle John, *"Even so, come, Lord Jesus"* (Revelation 22:20). Will this twentieth-century generation be that blessed generation? Will we be the ones to witness this great event?

> *37But as the days of Noe were, so shall also the coming of the Son of man be.*
> *38For as in the days that were before the flood they were eating and drinking, marrying and giving in marriage, until the day that Noe entered into the ark,*
> *39And knew not until the flood came, and took them all away; so shall also the coming of the Son of man be.*
> *(Matthew 24:37-39)*

> *11There is a generation that curseth their father, and doth not bless their mother.*

> [12]*There is a generation that are pure in their own eyes, and yet is not washed from their filthiness.*
> [13]*There is a generation, O how lofty are their eyes! and their eyelids are lifted up.*
> [14]*There is a generation, whose teeth are as swords.*   *(Proverbs 30:11-14)*

The Bible, as you can see, speaks very clearly about the wickedness of the generation that will exist at the time of the return of our Lord Jesus. But God also speaks of a righteous generation: *"For God is in the generation of the righteous"* (Psalm 14:5). While it is true that *"there is none righteous, no, not one"* (Romans 3:10), while it is true that like David of old we were all shaped in iniquity and conceived in sin (Psalm 51:5), and while none of us can claim any righteousness of our own, yet God's righteousness has been imputed to us through His Son, Jesus Christ. (See 2 Corinthians 5:21.) Therefore, we are a righteous generation. It is for just such a righteous generation that the Lord Jesus is coming back to this earth.

"One generation shall praise thy works to another," wrote David in Psalm 145:4. And Paul wrote to Timothy, his son in the Lord, *"I call to remembrance the unfeigned faith that is in thee, which dwelt first in thy grandmother Lois, and thy mother Eunice; and I am persuaded that in thee also"* (2 Timothy 1:5). God had not only called Lois and Eunice to His service, He had also laid His hand upon their offspring Timothy for the work of the ministry. How blessed it is to see the same faith that was in grandmother and mother passed on to their descendants. They had lived to see the reproduction of their lives in Christ bring forth a hundredfold through their posterity.

As I look back on the blessings of God that have been manifested in our family, and the move of God upon the earth in this twentieth century, I realize that I was born in the most exciting and challenging age of all preceding generations.

Though my parents were not preachers, they were among the pioneers of this century in this great move of God. Two of my older brothers, Henry and Winfred, were ministers of the Gospel. As a child I was taken to church regularly and was born again at the age of ten and filled with the Holy Spirit. Each morning before going to school, our family gathered together around the breakfast table for family prayer.

At times Dad or Mother would take me aside for prayer and counsel. It was a very strict Holiness home. Though my parents told me what they felt by God's Word to be right or wrong, they also taught me the fear of the Lord and the love of the Lord. I knew that whether I obeyed my parents or not, the Lord was watching and knew what I was doing. I was not really afraid of God as of a hard taskmaster, but rather of displeasing Him because I loved Him so much.

At the age of thirteen, in the city of Sanger, California, I was praying at the altar with some children who were seeking to be filled with the Holy Spirit, when suddenly the Lord truly filled me with a double portion of His Spirit. Several of us children were under the power of God for hours. Although I had been filled at the age of ten, I had not continued to speak in the heavenly language. God so beautifully restored this gift to me, and I have never stopped using the gift since then.

However, the neighbors were being disturbed by the noise of those wonderful services, and the police were called out at midnight. They came and took the preacher to jail, later returning to arrest the rest of us. But I was still walking on cloud nine and could not have cared less if we had been thrown into jail. After some time, we were all allowed to go on home. The next morning the preacher was also released. No one had to go to court.

I shall never forget that night as I lay under the power of the Holy Spirit speaking in a heavenly language. I saw the lost world in need of a Savior. It was at this time that I felt the call of God upon my life for His service. How beautiful it is to let the Holy Spirit pray through you. Let me encourage everyone who may be reading this book that as you continue to help others and to put to use what the Lord has given you, He shall flow through you like rivers of living water.

Our family moved from California to Texas when I was seventeen years of age. My co-worker, Alice Harris, and I began preaching at an early age, and were conducting revival meetings in East Texas. The highlight of our meetings together came in a service we held near Henderson, Texas. It was in an open-air tabernacle beside a cemetery.

Getting a crowd together to preach to in those days was no trouble. They came in wagons and cars, and many walked. The whole community seemed to be coming to the meetings. There were many saved and filled with the Spirit. The meeting broke through one night when three young men came forward and were saved. One of the young men, whose name was Leonard Wood, was also filled with the Holy Spirit. He was called into the ministry and has since been pastor of one of the leading churches in Dallas for years.

A revival like this was new to the people of this community, and it was producing quite a stir. Revival causes people to come face to face with themselves and with God. A number of hardened sinners were saved. To God be all the glory!

Our next meeting was an open-air meeting in Arp, Texas, near Tyler. No church had yet been established in Arp, but there was a group of people who were working toward organizing one there. After this meeting closed, two young men by the names of R. L. Davis and Don Stuckey who were just beginning their ministries came to continue the meetings. Here I met the man who was to become my husband.

But how did we meet? That story sounds like a fairy tale. A minister by the name of Bill Dunn was interested in my co-worker, Alice. I jokingly told him that if he were going to take my co-worker away from me (which he did!), he would have to find me another partner. Bill wanted to know his description, so I told him that he would have to be a preacher (since I was going to preach), and that I wanted him to sing and play the guitar and be good looking with dark, curly hair.

Although we were only joking and I surely didn't really expect him to find that "one and only" for me, within two weeks Bill called me and said that he had found my partner. I really laughed at such an idea.

"I was standing out in front of the First Assembly of God church in Fort Worth, where Brother F. D. Davis is pastor," Bill told me, "and out walked evangelist R. L. Davis. He just fit your description!" Then he announced that R. L. and his friend Don Stuckey were coming to Arp to carry on the meeting.

"That'll be all right," I said. "We're leaving town anyway." But it was not long until the opportunity came for Alice and me to attend their meeting.

There he stood, good looking and singing and playing the guitar. And he had black, curly hair! What more could you ask for? I felt embarrassed and hardly knew how to speak.

However, when God arranges something, He knows just how to do it. One of the ladies from the church invited Alice and me to spend the night with her, and then invited the boys over for breakfast. You would have thought it was all pre-arranged, but she certainly knew nothing of the previous conversations.

From there we began to date. When God puts a marriage together, it is beautiful. We were soon to marry and to organize our own evangelistic team.

6

If Two Walk Together

One may ask, "How can two people ever agree on everything?" Two people may not be able to agree on every situation, since we are individuals. However, it is of utmost importance that couples who are anticipating marriage be able to agree on the major issues of life. They need to have something in common, such as their life's work, desires, and ambitions. Two people who are joining together for the gospel ministry must indeed have the call of God upon their lives. Life at its best will have its problems and trials. To be in the gospel ministry, one will not only have the normal and usual problems, but also those of other people who are looking to him for help.

R. L. Davis also had the call of God upon his life and was just beginning his ministry as an evangelist. He was from a large Pentecostal family. However, he had only been saved a little over a year when we met. His mother was the daughter of a Baptist minister, and his father had a Methodist background. They lived on a farm and did not go to church much, but in the summertime, the Methodists and Baptists would get together for what they called a protracted meeting. R. L.'s mother had tried to tell the children about Jesus. She had a large picture of Christ on the wall which made a lasting impression on her son.

R. L. had gone forward to accept Christ as Savior, and was also filled with the Spirit. He had attended an open-air revival which was sponsored by his oldest brother, Doyle, who was the pastor of the First Assembly of God Church in Fort Worth, Texas. He soon felt the call of God upon his life for the ministry, so he began to read and study his Bible. He had wanted to attend Bible school, but did not get to go. It was not long until he and a co-worker, Don Stuckey, were out preaching and telling people all they had learned about God.

He had only begun to preach, and I, of course, had been raised in the Pentecostal movement and was already preaching. However, it was not long until he was a preacher in his own right. We were to enjoy many beautiful experiences in God's work together. It was not all easy by any means, but our blessings so far outweighed the hard times that we had no complaints.

We had married in the middle of the Depression when there was not any money. We did not have a car or anything. We had each other and the Lord. We were happy to be called of God to take this wonderful message to the world. Our ministry grew together. We had to trust the Lord for our meetings, our transportation, the food we ate, the clothes we wore, everything. But many of God's ministers could give similar testimonies of God's sustaining grace. He has never failed us.

One of our first revivals was in Alvarado, Texas. A group of people were meeting together in an old Free Will Baptist church that had to be propped up with a telephone pole. It was winter, and the rains had caused it to be muddy around the building. The church had "central" heating—a big pot-bellied stove in the middle of the building! Those who sat close were scorched, and those near the wall almost froze since some of the windowpanes were out.

We organized a chain of prayer with eleven people promising to pray an hour a day. Needless to say, revival broke out. There were forty-two saved and nineteen filled with the Holy Ghost, many of whom had been hardened sinners. The revival touched the town.

This was during the time when President Franklin Roosevelt had closed the banks. The people did not have any money. It was not hard to trust the Lord in those days since people did not have anywhere else to turn. It seems that many times when people prosper, they do not feel their need for God. The people took up an offering of chickens and sold them to raise our love offering. It amounted to $14.00 for a four-week campaign. We felt happy and well rewarded for the many souls who had found Christ.

The Davis family had been deprived of their father when R. L. was eleven years old. He had developed a serious blood disease called pernicious anemia. However, Doyle, the older brother, was instrumental in leading his father to the Lord before his death and seeing him filled with the Spirit.

Doyle and his family tell many stories of revival meetings in new areas. They preached in brush arbors and school houses with no one to sponsor them but the Lord. There were a number of occasions when they had to pray in each meal.

One day one of the children said, "I want some cookies! Would God send cookies?" This was a difficult question for the family to answer because they needed food, period. They had gotten up that morning with nothing in the house to eat. What were they to do? What would they tell the children? They were standing looking out the window when they saw a man coming down the road carrying a large basket of food. He came directly to their house. On top of the large basket of groceries lay a package of cookies.

The Lord surely cares for His own. He hears even the cry of His little children. He sees the sparrows when they fall. He cares for the lilies of the field. He has promised to supply all our needs according to His riches in glory by Christ Jesus.

Doyle tells of the time he and his family stayed in a house near Huntsville, Texas. They were preaching the miracle-working power of the Lord. They always came in from the services tired and thirsty. On one occasion they had drawn a bucket of water and left it on the porch to cool. While they were gone to the service, some man slipped up to the water pail and poured strychnine into it. When they came in from the meeting, they went directly to the water pail and drank freely from it. The man stood in the distance to watch and see how it affected them. When nothing happened, the man was so convinced of his sin he later confessed it; otherwise, no one would have ever known about it. Has not God said in His Word, *"if they drink any deadly thing, it shall not hurt them"* (Mark 16:18)?

There were six of the Davis boys and three girls. Now all have been saved and filled with the Spirit. Another of the boys, Sherman, has also been called to the preaching ministry. But then, are not all of God's children called into the ministry in one way or another?

When the Lord took their father home, R. L. remembers hearing him sing, "He will keep His words with you, yes, He will." I am sure he must have asked the Lord that his family be an unbroken circle around the throne. Today, we have not only seen this immediate family come to the Lord, but also many of the children and grandchildren are saved, and several are in full-time ministry.

Doyle had been able to lead his father to the Lord and was privileged to see him baptized with the Holy Spirit. From that time on, other members of the family began to yield their lives to God. It is blessed to see the chain reaction in a family. Doyle and his wife, Addie, were parents of ten children. Four of their sons are in the ministry, two daughters married preachers, and the other children are busily engaged in the work of God in their local churches.

The family looked to their older brother, Doyle, as sort of the priest of the family. His influence will live on, not only in the lives of his own family, but throughout the state of Texas and other parts of the country as well. He served as the District Superintendent of the Texas District of the Assemblies of God for ten years. He also served as the first President of Southwestern Assemblies of God College in Waxahachie, Texas.

Many of God's great servants have enjoyed the influence of a godly home. We think of John and Charles Wesley, the founders of the great Methodist church, who were profoundly influenced by their godly mother. Adoniram Judson, the great missionary to India, came from a minister's home. The list could go on and on of the many great men of God who had godly forebears.

I might add here that having godly parents does not necessarily make a person a Christian. Each person must be responsible to God for his own life and standing with Him. But as it is written, *"For unto whomsoever much is given, of him shall be much required: and to whom men have committed much, of him they will ask the more"* (Luke 12:48). The responsibility is ours; we cannot escape it. We praise God for His grace which has reached down into the lowest pit and saved those who had no such upbringing.

Jesus came into the world to save sinners. We are all sinners. *"There is none righteous, no not one"* (Romans 3:10). Jesus saved a woman whom everyone knew to be a sinner. She loved Him so much she sat at His feet washing them with her tears and wiping them with the hair of her head. Jesus said of her, *"Wherefore I say...Her sins, which are many, are forgiven; for she loved much: but to whom little is forgiven, the same loveth little"* (Luke 7:47).

Our brother Doyle has since gone on to his reward, leaving a great testimony of the love of Jesus. At the end he called his family around his bed and told them good-bye, closed his eyes, and went to be with Jesus. The sting of death has been removed from the Christian. The day of his death becomes his coronation day.

7

One Generation to Another

One generation shall praise thy works to another. —Psalm 145:4

I could truly fill a volume with our many experiences in the gospel work. We were privileged to build and pastor six churches, and to pastor others we did not build. This ministry led us into many places in the States and around the world. We held city-wide campaigns in auditoriums and tents.

I relate some of these incidents only to say that it has been my happy privilege to watch the work of God's Spirit in many phases of the ministry. I have watched it grow from its simple beginnings in the brush arbor days, from meetings in school houses and missions, to what it is today with its beautiful new churches and cathedrals around the world. But wherever the Spirit of God has given the right-of-way, revival continues. If it has cooled down, it is from lack of prayer and dedication and loss of faith in the miracle-working power of the Lord. Thank God, there is a remnant who still believe in and who are still seeing the power of God in action today.

I have lived to see God take the children He has given us, Burnie, Gerald, and Rick, and lay His hands on them for the gospel ministry. These young people still have the fire and zeal for God, and they are being used as pastors and evangelists, some in great campaigns on foreign soil. Now God is also calling our grandchildren and many of our nieces and nephews.

One Generation to Another

I have seen four generations, beginning with my parents who were among the first to be filled with the Spirit in 1906. We have no choice but to respond to God's call upon our lives. *"For unto whomsoever much is given, of him shall much be required"* (Luke 12:48). This is a great heritage, and it must be carried on. Each generation is responsible for the generation in which they live. The present generation could indeed be the last generation before the second coming of the Lord.

> *[2]The harvest is great, but the laborers are few: pray ye therefore the Lord of the harvest, that he would send forth laborers into his harvest.* *(Luke 10:2)*

The last church we were to build and pioneer was in El Cajon, California, a suburb of San Diego. We had put up our big gospel tent in this beautiful valley teeming with people. God had given us a great revival, and the people were saying, "Let's build a church."

We found an ideal piece of property in the central part of the city. Through His miracle-working power, God made it possible for us to obtain this property. Yes, I think we may have been too old to tackle such a job—if fifty is too old. Winter was coming on. How long can you hold a crowd under a tent? We had to find other quarters. We moved the crowd to three different locations before we were finally able to build a chapel.

We could not borrow the money for construction because the loan companies said our church had to be five years old before we could qualify for a loan. But God sent us a Presbyterian contractor and loan officer who said that the Lord had impressed his heart to build our church. He drew the plans for the chapel and obtained a loan for us. We were soon in our own building.

Revival broke out and we were never at a loss for a crowd. Denominational people were coming and being filled with the Holy Spirit. *"The Lord added to the church daily such as should be saved"* (Acts 2:47).

At one time my husband was having morning prayer meetings in our church with several denominational preachers meeting with him. We heard them praying and speaking in tongues together. Truly, this was a new day! God was bringing His church together by the power of the Holy Spirit. At one time a great charismatic conference was held in the First Presbyterian Church in downtown San Diego. Spirit-filled denominational ministers came together and shared their testimonies.

We did not make any distinctions by what church we belonged to, we were just Christians. Someone has said that it does not make any difference what the first name is as long as the last name is Christian. God is calling hungry people everywhere who are desirous of more from Him.

My husband was active in our city's ministerial alliance where he had become acquainted with the president of the association, the Rev. Harold Christmann, pastor of the First Christian Church. Their hearts became knitted together, and they became prayer partners, first in Brother Christmann's church, then in ours, as he felt he had more liberty in our church to pray. Brother Christmann had been attending "The Camp Farthest Out," a group of people who were really reaching out to God. He had been praying for the sick and seeing some results.

One day Brother Christmann asked my husband what the secret of his success was in his meetings. He explained to him about the baptism of the Holy Spirit. Brother Christmann immediately said, "I have the Holy Spirit."

My husband did not argue the point with him, but simply replied, "Sure you do;

no one can be saved without the operation of the Holy Spirit." It surprised the man that my husband would agree with him.

"However," my husband continued, "*He dwelleth with you, and shall be in you'* (John 14:17), which suggests something more. There is an added dimension of power called the baptism of the Holy Ghost."

"It's funny," said Brother Christmann, "I hadn't noticed that before." Then he added, "Well, pray for me. I would like to have this power."

After a series of prayer meetings in which each prayed for the other before they started their day's activities, God wonderfully filled this Christian brother with the Holy Spirit. It was not long until his entire family had been filled. God is still using this man in his newly-found, Spirit-filled walk.

We ministered in this lovely city of El Cajon for eight years and saw the work grow constantly. However, little did we realize that this constant drive and compulsion was taking its toll on my husband's body. We felt that it was up to us to win the world for Christ. I am sure that without this zeal little could have been accomplished.

Regardless, Paul said, *"We have this treasure in earthen vessels"* (2 Colossians 4:7). Earthen vessels wear out. We wonder why the lives of so many of God's great soldiers of the cross sometimes are seemingly cut short. Why can't we all live out our years as we count time?

Paul wrote to the church at Philippi:

25Yet I supposed it necessary to send to you Epaphroditus, my brother, and companion in labor, and fellow soldier, but your messenger, and he that ministered to my wants.

²⁶*For he longed after you all, and was full of heaviness, because that ye had heard that he had been sick.*
²⁷*For indeed he was sick nigh unto death: but God had mercy on him; and not on him only, but on me also, lest I should have sorrow upon sorrow.*
³⁰*Because for the work of Christ he was nigh unto death, not regarding his life, to supply your lack of service toward me.*
(Philippians 2:25-27, 30)

This was Paul's co-worker in the gospel ministry who had become very ill because he had pushed his body beyond what it could take. But God was merciful and healed him. How many of God's servants have we seen do the same thing?

R. L. had never been sick many days in his life, but he felt the burden of the world upon his shoulders. As far as he was concerned, the salvation of the world depended solely upon him. There is a burden and a divine compulsion within the hearts of God's true ministers in the world today that will not let them stop as long as there is breath within their bodies.

R. L. had a coronary heart attack and was very ill. However, prayer was made in his behalf across the country. God brought him through this crisis and gave him six more years of fruitful ministry before He took him home. Death came suddenly on a Sunday morning in Palestine, Texas, where he had grown up as a boy. He was to have begun a revival that morning, but instead, God promoted him to his heavenly home.

What was I to do now? My world had suddenly come to an end. Another grave had been opened. The last song had been sung by the graveside: "I Will Meet You over Yonder, Just Outside the Eastern Gate." For some reason I had been left.

The Lord had said, *"Occupy till I come"* (Luke 19:13). We must go on. The morning of my husband's passing, the Lord had given me a dream based upon the Scripture in Acts 2:39: *"The promise is unto you, and to your children."* The emphasis of the dream seemed to be upon the promises of God. God let me know that His promises were for me and my children in this dark hour. He would never leave us nor forsake us. *"Yea, though I walk through the valley of the shadow of death, I will fear no evil: for thou art with me; thy rod and thy staff they comfort me"* (Psalm 23:4).

Before he passed away, R. L. had received an opportunity to go to Colon, Panama, for a campaign at the invitation of Wayne Turnbull, a missionary stationed there. He had looked forward to going; however, he was never able to make that trip. Burnie, our oldest son, and I went. God gave us a great campaign there. Burnie preached the night services, and I spoke in the day. It was truly a blessed experience for me. Many were saved, filled, and healed.

The divine compulsion within still says, "God is not through with you yet!" I know the boys feel the same way.

8

It Won't Be Long Now

And it shall come to pass afterward, that I will pour out my spirit on all flesh; and your sons and your daughters shall prophesy, your old men shall dream dreams, your young men shall see visions. And also upon the servants and upon the handmaids in those days will I pour out my spirit. —Joel 2:28-29

Two months after the passing of my husband, God gave the following vision or dream to our second son, Gerald. Here is Gerald's account of that dream as he remembered it:

There I was, floating over the earth, bodily, held by the hand of a Man. I could see the land and sea below, much the same as when I had flown in the giant jets across land and sea. I asked, "Where are we going?" He answered, "You will see." I noticed that my love for this Man was unusual, and I wondered at His identity.

I thought, Should He turn me loose, I would fall. I began to wonder at my security when I decided to try His foot, so I stepped on it with His approving smile. His foot was like a rock. I told myself, This must be the Lord! He is a sure foundation. There is no need to fear.

As we continued, I found myself in space. Here there was a dead silence for a short time until we arrived at the gates of heaven. There was a tall fence with large posts that extended into the sky. I could not see the top. Suddenly there were seven men walking directly toward me. One of them was my father whom we had just recently laid to rest. He reached his hands through the fence, caught me by the arm, and exclaimed, "Oh, Gerald!"

Then suddenly beside me stood my mother and my two brothers, Burnie and Rick. There were three of us boys born to R. L. and Clara Davis. We were also gospel ministers and had recently been traveling as evangelists. Our father had left us early one Sunday morning without saying good-bye.

It seemed strange to me that my father should return to greet us. How our hearts rejoiced over this rare occasion to be allowed the opportunity to converse about things we would have liked to talk about had we known he was leaving us. He looked so happy and healthy, and he talked about heaven and its unspeakable beauty. He had admonished us to continue in the ministry God had given us. One thing I shall never forget is that he emphasized the fact that, "It won't be long until we will all be together again."

I recognized the other men who were with him as angels who were his escorts. Suddenly one of them said, "We must be going now." They turned and went back towards that celestial city which I could see in the background. Dad had his hands lifted, shouting and praising the Lord. We were left holding to the gates and weeping because he had left us again. We had to return to the earth as our jobs were not yet finished.

Then I awoke, actually weeping and praising the Lord. It all seemed so real. I think I must have felt something of what the apostle Paul felt when he said, *"I knew a man in Christ above fourteen years ago, (whether in the body, I cannot tell; or whether out of the body, I cannot tell: God knoweth;) such an one caught up to the third heaven"* (2 Corinthians 12:2). I felt like I had been allowed a brief visit to heaven, if only to the gates.

I had been reared in a minister's home, was now engaged as a pastor, and had preached the power of the resurrection and life after death. However, from some unseen force as I had stood by the graveside of this great man, my own father whom we admired so much, had come the passing thought, Is it all really true, this life after death?

I immediately began to remember the Scriptures and the many promises in God's Word:

>*¹Let not your heart be troubled: ye believe in God, believe also in me.*
>*²In my Father's house are many mansions: if it were not so, I would have told you. I go to prepare a place for you.*
>*³And if I go and prepare a place for you, I will come again, and receive you unto*

*myself; that where I am, there ye may be
also.*   *(John 14:1-3)*

I read the great resurrection chapter of 1
Corinthians:

*¹³But if there be no resurrection of the
dead, then is Christ not risen:
¹⁴And if Christ be not risen, then is our
preaching vain, and your faith is also
vain.
¹⁵Yea, and we are found false witnesses of
God; because we have testified of God that
he raised up Christ: whom he raised not
up, if so be that the dead rise not.
¹⁶For if the dead rise not, then is not
Christ raised:
¹⁷And if Christ be not raised, your faith is
vain; ye are yet in your sins.
¹⁸Then they also which are fallen asleep in
Christ are perished.
¹⁹If in this life only we have hope in Christ,
we are of all men most miserable.
²⁰But now is Christ risen from the dead,
and become the firstfruits of them that
slept.*   *(1 Corinthians 15:13-20)*

9

Cherished Testimonies

For God is in the generation of the righteous.
                                    —Psalm 14:5

From Burnie, our oldest son, we have a portion of his personal testimony, part of which previously has appeared in print:[1]

As a child I remember that our home was a home of prayer. I was raised in a Pentecostal parsonage. I slept on church benches, and my playmates were church kids. This was all I knew until I was a teenager. At that time, my brother Gerald

---

[1] Burnie Davis, "They Cherish Their Pentecostal Heritage," *Testimony* (Second Quarter, 1965), 10-16.

97

and I decided we would seek other company and see what the world had to offer. We got away from God and caused our parents a lot of concern. However, we were not able to enjoy our "freedom" for long, because there was such a bombardment of prayer going up in our behalf, we could no longer resist.

I found my mother on her knees one morning around 2:00 A.M. praying, "God, save my son." I tried to slip in the house and go to bed without awakening anyone. However, my parents had not gone to sleep. I crawled into bed and covered up my head to drown out her prayers, but there was no stopping her. Under extreme conviction I surrendered my life to God and decided to go to Bible school to prepare for the ministry. My parents had neither encouraged nor discouraged their sons to go into the ministry. They did, however, make us feel that the call of God was the highest call on earth.

At the age of eighteen, I was conducting my first revival. Gerald, my brother, had pioneered and pastored his first church in Annaville, near Corpus Christi, Texas. My younger brother Rick had been attending Southern California College in Costa Mesa, California, and was preparing for the ministry. All three of us boys are active in the gospel ministry.

I will always remember the first revival Gerald and I held together. We had borrowed a tent and had put it up in a little town near Corpus Christi. We had also borrowed a piano and were really going to shake the city for God. However, a storm came up, the tent was torn to shreds, and the piano was left sitting in the water. We had only one convert, a little boy. We felt as if our whole effort was a complete failure. But years later, we met this boy who was now grown and a pastor of a church. Truly, our efforts are not in vain in the Lord.

Burnie's testimony as well as those of his brothers have touched many lives for God's purposes. God has used these young godly men as evangelists and pastors. They have all served as missionary evangelists in foreign countries preaching to masses and seeing many miracles of healing and salvation. To God be the glory! God is raising up young men and women all over the world to take this message of the kingdom around the globe.

For example, we think of Talmage and Marjorie Butler. Talmage is the son of Edna and Coy Butler, a sister and brother-in-law of my husband. These young people were missionaries, first to the Bahamas, and then to Senegal, West Africa. They stand tall in the hearts of those with whom they worked.

Talmage and Marjorie and their son, Stevie, were to return to Africa for their third term. They had decided to make one last trip to their beloved Bahamas. Their plane disappeared somewhere in the waters between Miami and the Bahama Islands. But even as this happened, their spirits were ushered to that heavenly shore to be with the Lord.

Tragedy? Yes, it seems such a loss. We cannot understand many things that happen on earth. But our loss is heaven's gain. They were driven with that divine compulsion that would not let them stay home and enjoy a more serene life. They always felt that they had to win one more soul for Christ. However, today there is a church in Senegal which stands as a memorial to their work. Some people do more in their few short years than many of us get done in a whole lifetime. The full story of this heroic, dedicated couple can be read in the book, *Africa Is Waiting.*[2]

---

[2]Sue Schaeffer, *Africa Is Waiting* (Grand Rapids, MI: Baker Book House, 1970).

10

Who Are These Charismatics?

Today there are charismatic Lutherans, Catholics, Episcopalians, Baptists, Presbyterians, Methodists, and those from many other denominations. "What does this mean?" one may ask. "Who are these people?" These are those who have been filled with the Holy Spirit according to Acts 2:4, many of whom are still remaining in their respective churches. All of these may not agree on every phase of doctrine or manner of worship, but all agree on the work of the Holy Spirit, and all regard "speaking in tongues" as being literal and for the present time.

Webster's New Edition Dictionary defines the word *charisma* as "a divinely inspired gift (as of prophesying); a special magnetic quality of leadership." We hear this word used today by many people to describe someone who is especially gifted or personable: "He (or she) has charisma." This definition in *Webster's* means that to have charisma or to be charismatic is to be "divinely gifted."

Although there are Pentecostal denominations or fellowships, Pentecost is not a denomination. The Holy Spirit anointing came on the particular feast day of the Jews called Pentecost. Consequently, Pentecost has since then been associated with this blessed experience of the baptism of the Holy Spirit which was first manifested on that day. The world did not understand the baptism of the Holy Ghost then, and it does not understand it now. Truly it is a divine phenomenon. Those whom the Holy Spirit empowered on that day were accused of being drunk; evidently they were in a pretty high emotional state. It is hard to keep from reacting strongly to such power. However, the baptism is more than merely an impassioned incident; otherwise, once the initial emotionalism subsided, the experience would lose its effect, but this does not happen.

The Holy Spirit comes to abide, to empower. *"Ye shall receive power, after that the Holy Ghost is come upon you: and ye shall be witnesses...unto the uttermost part of the earth"* (Acts 1:8). When the Holy Spirit of God has come upon us, He is there when we need Him to empower us to witness, to pray, to heal the sick, to cast out devils. He is there to be used in operating the gifts of the Spirit, according to the measure of our faith and our yieldedness to Him.

The "charismatic movement," as it is called today, is the manifestation of the same power that came to the early church. But the church as a whole failed to participate and operate in this power of the Holy Spirit until the turn of the twentieth century. At that time a renewal of interest in the Holy Spirit baptism began to manifest throughout the world. Presently, many in denominational churches are receiving this experience. God must do a quick work! Time is running out! Man's feeble efforts —even our great political, social, and educational systems—are failing to stem the tide of wickedness and unconcern.

We thank God for the media, for radio, television, and the printed page, by which the Word of God is being proclaimed across the land. We thank God for modern, efficient transportation, such as automobiles, airplanes, and boats. They, too, are being used by God to transport gospel literature around the world. But as marvelous as these modern means of communication and transportation are, they must still be operated by people of God with a vision to evangelize the world. We must have a message of deliverance to be able to heal the sick and perform miracles in the name of Jesus. *"These signs shall follow them that believe"* (Mark 16:17).

The Pentecostal experience began to break outside the boundaries of the traditional Pentecostal church between the years 1950 and 1960. Many denominational churches began to feel the impact. Some of their ministers began to receive this experience, and when they openly declared it to their churches, many times it caused them to lose their congregations and their credentials. Still, many of the members did begin to reread the book of Acts and to ask, "Why can't we still have the same results today that those early disciples had back then?"

God began to fill these hungry hearts with the same experience as manifested in

Acts chapters 2, 10, and 19. It is obvious from chapters 12 through 14 of Paul's first letter to the Corinthians that the church in Corinth manifested the gifts of the Spirit. If the power and gifts of the Holy Spirit were necessary to get the early church started, why would they not also be necessary today to prepare the church to fulfill the Great Commission?

When this revival of "speaking in tongues" began to invade the Roman Catholic Church, we were all amazed. In 1966 Catholic laymen who were associated with Duquesne University in Pittsburgh, Pennsylvania, began meeting in prayer meetings and seeking God. As a result, several received the Pentecostal experience. They began to testify to the students of Duquesne University, the University of Notre Dame, and elsewhere. The experience spread. Today it is estimated that there are nearly one-half million Catholic Pentecostals.

Who Are These Charismatics?

One young lady, a member of a certain Catholic church in Houston, was so excited about her new-found experience with the Lord and being filled with the Holy Spirit, she shared it eagerly with a friend. I overheard her telling the friend that she hoped to soon be able to see some special prayer services in her church. She explained to me that since they were now able to read the Bible for themselves, Catholics were beginning to realize that this was the way the early church started, and that their church had just slipped away from the original pattern.

Many of these people seem to be able to remain in their churches, hoping and praying that others will see the light also. They are praying for their pastors to become enlightened and are burdened for their friends and church. Some are being tolerated while others are being ostracized. We are wondering how long this situation can go on. People will finally have to make a stand one way or the other. Persecution will usually draw the line.

David Wilkerson, author of *The Cross and the Switchblade,* is convinced that this persecution will come. Not only is the Holy Spirit calling out a people and bringing about a certain amount of unity in some areas, but persecution may be the furnace that will melt the body of Christ together. The lukewarm will be spewed out of the Lord's mouth. The choice will be Christ or Antichrist. The bride of Christ will have her garments washed in the blood of the Lamb. Her garments will be righteousness, not defiled with the sins of this world.

It will take more than emotions or exhilarated feelings to help us to stand in the day of extreme persecution and tribulation. By this I do not mean to imply that the church is destined to go through the Great Tribulation and the reign of the Antichrist. However, through the ages the saints have undergone great persecution and tribulation. Many are undergoing great suffering in various areas of the world today. *"Yea, and all that will live godly in Christ Jesus shall suffer persecution"* (2 Timothy 3:12). His church will be refined by the fires of Pentecost and the fires of persecution. The lukewarm will not be ready for the Rapture of the church. We need to be rooted and grounded in the Word of God.

My sons Burnie and Rick have been conducting crusades in Mexico, Honduras, Nicaragua, Guatemala, and throughout Central America. They have been astonished to find so many Catholic charismatics attending their meetings. They have found it easy not only to preach the message of salvation and divine healing, but also to tell the people in public meetings about the Pentecostal experience of speaking in other tongues. The hearts of the people are receptive, and many are being filled with the Holy Spirit. Jesus said, *"I must work the works of him that sent me, while it is day: the night cometh, when no man can work"* (John 9:4).

The charismatic movement is growing so rapidly that it cannot be ignored. Scarcely a church exists which has not been affected. It is causing quite an upheaval in many denominations. But what spiritual revolution such as this will not rock the boat? Anything which seems new to people brings criticism. Christ certainly disrupted the established church of His day.

> *[34]Think not that I am come to send peace on earth: I came not to send peace, but a sword...*
> *[36]A man's foes shall be they of his own household.   (Matthew 10:34, 36)*

> *[9]Whom shall he teach knowledge? and whom shall he make to understand doctrine? them that are weaned from the milk, and drawn from the breasts.*
> *   (Isaiah 28:9)*

*⁶My people are destroyed for lack of knowl-
edge.*   *(Hosea 4:6)*

It is important what one believes. It
must be the whole Word of God. That is
why God has set in the church apostles,
prophets, evangelists, teachers, and pastors
for the maturing and perfecting of the
saints. (See Ephesians 4:11-13.) We wish
we could say that all who call themselves
shepherds were indeed true shepherds. But
Jeremiah 50:6 says: *"My people hath been
lost sheep: their shepherds have caused
them to go astray, they have turned them
away on the mountains."* Still, God gives
this promise:

*⁴I will set up shepherds over them which
shall feed them: and they shall fear no
more, nor be dismayed, neither shall they
be lacking, saith the Lord.*
                              (Jeremiah 23:4)

Three points are essential to a clear
understanding of what God is doing today

through the power of the Holy Spirit at work in the church. The following discussion of these three points is taken from an article written by Fred Smolchuch which appeared in the *Pentecostal Evangel* of July 18, 1976, and is used by permission:

First, there must be a time of growing and maturing in the Word of God. We do believe that spiritual balance is very important. All truths relate one to another and cannot be isolated. If any one truth is isolated and elevated above all other truths, this can only lead to confusion and disillusionment. The well-grounded Christian accepts the whole truth. He will not side step any part of God's truth. His truth may bring us material gain or bring us into trying circumstances. His truth will lead us to knowledge and maturity.

[32]*Ye shall know the truth, and the truth shall make you free.* (John 8:32)

> *¹¹When I was a child, I spake as a child, I understood as a child, I thought as a child: but when I became a man, I put away childish things.*
>
> *(1 Corinthians 13:11)*

God has had to lead His people step by step.

> *¹⁰For precept must be upon precept, precept upon precept; line upon line, here a little, and there a little:*
> *¹¹For with stammering lips and another tongue will he speak to this people.*
> *¹²To whom he said, This is the rest wherewith ye may cause the weary to rest; and this is the refreshing: yet they would not hear.* *(Isaiah 28:10-12)*

Second, God does reveal additional truths to us from time to time. Truth has been there all the time, as God has not changed. Man has been blinded to it. He has been taught it is not for our day. When the light of the glorious Gospel shines into our lives, it becomes a divine revelation to us. There is a time of spiritual growing up and maturity. *"If our gospel be hid, it is hid to them that are lost"* (2 Corinthians 4:3). It is a great day in the life of anyone who awakens to the fact that all the promises of God are for us and for our day.

However, with every new spiritual revelation, there has always remained a danger of an overemphasis upon certain truths without a proper balance to the Word of God. What has disturbed many is the fluctuation in doctrinal emphasis and position. This indeed is quite understandable from people coming from so many denominational backgrounds. A spirit of love and understanding will help us to be patient with the little sheep who are so tender and young.

Third, spirituality, prayer, worship, and spiritual gifts are all important. Yet, spirituality without discipline becomes hypocrisy. Prayer without repentance, humility, and faith is anemic and hopeless. Worship without obedience and involvement in God's work is like smoke in God's nostrils. Spiritual gifts without spiritual fruit are weak and ineffective. There must be a balance.

Christ alone has the answer. He is the Great Shepherd. He is the Door. He is *"the way, the truth, and the life"* (John 14:6). All revelation of truth flows from Him like the many rays of the sun.

> *⁶If we say that we have fellowship with him, and walk in darkness, we lie, and do not the truth:*
> *⁷But if we walk in the light, as he is in the light, we have fellowship one with another, and the blood of Jesus Christ his Son cleanseth us from all sin. (1 John 1:6-7)*

11

His Banner Over Us Is Love

He brought me to the banqueting house, and his banner over me was love.
                    —Song of Solomon 2:4

Who is she that looketh forth as the morning, fair as the moon, clear as the sun, and terrible as an army with banners?
                    —Song of Solomon 6:10

Christ is making up His army. The orders are, "Charge!" Ours is more than a defensive warfare against the works of Satan. We need a united front.

> *[11]Put on the whole armor of God, that ye may be able to stand against the wiles of the devil.*
> *[12]For we wrestle not against flesh and blood, but against principalities, against powers, against the rulers of the darkness of this world, against spiritual wickedness in high places.   (Ephesians 6:11-12)*

Many times soldiers who have fought side by side on the battlefield become fast friends for life because there is a certain affinity and comradeship that they shared together in the foxhole that binds them together for the rest of their days. Likewise, Christians in Communist countries and in concentration camps surely must forfeit their denominational labels and become just Christians and brothers in Christ. When we suffer together, there is a special kind of love which is developed one for the other.

> *[1]Behold, what manner of love the Father hath bestowed upon us, that we should be*

*called the sons of God: therefore the world
knoweth us not, because it knew him not.
²Beloved, now are we the sons of God and
it doth not yet appear what we shall be:
but we know that, when he shall appear,
we shall be like him; for we shall see him
as he is.*   *(1 John 3:1-2)*

"One will not find the perfect church
while on this earth. The New Testament
churches were not perfect, but they had a
standard, and it was not imperfection. Let
us tune our instruments to the standard
pitch of the New Testament church."[1]

*³It was needful for me to write unto you,
and exhort you that you should earnestly
contend for the faith which was once delivered unto the saints.*   *(Jude 3)*

Some criticize this charismatic movement as being ecumenical in nature. They
say that those who are involved in it are

---

[1]Vance Havner, *Why Not Just Be Christians?* (Old
Tappan, NJ: Revell, 1964), 13.

attempting to form a world church. This is not so. What they are doing is recognizing the unity of believers. *"The Spirit beareth witness with our Spirit that we are the children of God"* (Romans 8:16).

This true unity of believers certainly cannot be accomplished by some international "super church" such as the one now being formed in an attempt to bring about the unity of the churches of the world through compromise, letting down Bible standards so as not to offend anyone. Such a "church" will be a roost for every foul bird and unclean spirit imaginable. God commands, *"Come out from among them, and be ye separate"* (2 Corinthians 6:17). Judgment is coming to the great whore of Revelation, chapter 17. She will align herself for awhile with the Antichrist.

It is the Holy Spirit of God which will bring the body of Christ together. We will have one common denominator, the Person of the Lord Jesus Christ. *"And I, if I be lifted up from the earth, will draw all men unto me"* (John 12:32). The Holy Spirit is the agent who is gathering the bride together, even as Abraham's servant found the bride for Isaac, a type of Christ. (See Genesis 24.)

How we would love to see every church catch on fire for God. However, we know that there will be many who will be satisfied to remain in the lukewarm Laodicean church of Revelation 3, content and increased with goods and in need of nothing. We see Jesus standing on the outside saying, *"Behold, I stand at the door, and knock: if any man hear my voice, and open the door, I will come in to him, and will sup with him, and he with me"* (Revelation 3:20). In each of the churches of Revelation we see a remnant who have not defiled their garments, but who are overcomers.

The Philadelphia church, though persecuted, has before her an open door. To that church Christ says, *"Because thou hast kept the word of my patience, I also will keep thee from the hour of temptation which shall come upon all the world, to try them that dwell upon the earth. Behold I come quickly: hold fast that which thou hast, that no man take thy crown"* (Revelation 3:10-11).

While attending a meeting not long ago, two women received almost the same vision, or prophetic words. The vision was of a large wheat field, blowing gently in the breeze. While wondering about the significance of the vision, it was revealed to one of the ladies that this was the wind of the Holy Spirit gently blowing upon the harvest of this world, which was ready to be reaped. She saw a sickle lying beside the field. She wanted to pick it up and start cutting with it, but she was warned that she was not ready for that yet.

"When shall I use the sickle, Lord?" she asked.

He answered, "Wait until you are ready to thrust it in love, for then you won't bruise the wheat. If the harvest is reaped without love behind the scythe, the grain will surely be bruised and trampled to the ground. Only love can be tender enough to preserve all."

The life of Christ must be working in a person motivating him to reap, for only the Lord has the agape love which is worthy to wield the sickle. No wonder Christ rebuked the church at Ephesus in the book of Revelation saying to them: *"I have somewhat against thee, because thou hast left thy first love"* (Revelation 2:4). Three times the Lord asked Peter, *"Simon, son of Jonas, lovest thou me?"* And three times He commanded him, *"Feed my sheep"* (John 21:15, 16, 17). God's harvest has been bruised and hurt by many well-meaning people who have not shown a spirit of love and forgiveness, but who have been quick to judge and criticize the little lambs for whom Christ died. He died for the whole world, regardless of race, creed, color, or social standing. How can we judge another man's servant? (See Romans 14:4.)

> *[2]The harvest truly is great, but the laborers are few: pray ye therefore the Lord of the harvest, that he would send forth laborers into his harvest.* *(Luke 10:2)*

12

You Ain't Seen Nothin' Yet!

C an the church of the twentieth century truly expect apostolic results such as a great outpouring of the Holy Spirit with power to perform miracles as experienced by the early church? Many Christians would like to experience such apostolic results in their ministry. They would like to have revival fires sweep through their families and churches. However, many forget that results like this come from apostolic faith. Can these same experiences happen in our present generation, or did all that end with the early church?

"Has the church age ended? Has the Holy Spirit been taken out of the world? Has God's plan changed? If so, when and where did He indicate the change? There is no scriptural intimation of a change in God's plan during the church age, nor before He comes to take His bride away. Why should we merely assume that there has been a change in God's plan? Why not believe the promises of God are *Yea and Amen'* (2 Corinthians 1:20) to us who believe, and available for today, as well as for those who lived closer to the time when they were uttered."[1]

When was there ever a time when we needed an added anointing of power more than in the age in which we now live?

[1] Ralph Riggs, *The Spirit Himself* (Springfield, MO: Gospel Publishing House, 1949), 95.

Before He left, Christ told His disciples:

[12]Verily, verily, I say unto you, He that believeth on me, the works that I do shall he do also; and greater works than these shall he do; because I go unto my Father. [13]And whatsoever ye shall ask in my name, that will I do, that the Father may be glorified in the Son. [14]If ye shall ask any thing in my name, I will do it. *(John 14:12-14)*

This Scripture passage staggers the mind of man. Did the disciples do greater works than Christ? Was this promise just for the apostolic age? I am convinced that Christ meant exactly what He said: that when He had gone, the Holy Spirit would come upon the church and empower us to do the same works He had done, only on a much larger scale and scope. Christ could only be in one place at a time, but through the power of the Holy Spirit, He can manifest Himself throughout the whole world in a mighty army of Spirit-filled believers.

> *²⁴Verily, verily, I say unto you, Except a corn of wheat fall into the ground and die, it abideth alone: but if it die, it bringeth forth much fruit.*   *(John 12:24)*

It was necessary that Christ die and be raised again. When He arose and went back to the Father, the Holy Spirit came and rested upon His church for the purpose of fulfilling the Great Commission.

> *¹⁹Behold, I give unto you power to tread upon serpents and scorpions, and over all the powers of the enemy; and nothing shall by any means hurt you.*   *(Luke 10:19)*

A. B. Simpson, founder of the Christian and Missionary Alliance, said at the turn of the century that he expected a restoration of all the gifts of the Holy Spirit and a mighty sweeping revival before the return of the Lord to the earth. Yes, it is true that we are living in a time of apostasy. The church as a whole is in a lukewarm, self-satisfied state.

> [37]But as the days of Noe were, so shall also the coming of the Son of man be.
> [38]For as in the days that were before the flood they were eating and drinking, marrying and giving in marriage, until the day that Noe entered into the ark;
> [39]And knew not until the flood came, and took them all away; so shall the coming of the Son of man be.   (Matthew 24:37-39)

In the last days, wickedness will abound, and men's hearts will grow worse. However, in the midst of this, the church is crying out to God, "One more time, Lord, send revival. Revive Your work in the midst of the years." (See Habakkuk 3:2). The clouds of darkness are gathering; the church will cry, *"Even so, come, Lord Jesus"* (Revelation 22:20).

The apostolic church began on the day of Pentecost in full bloom with all the gifts of the Spirit. Persecution and tribulation could not stop her. That divine compulsion was there. The believers went everywhere preaching the Gospel. They went forth to take this Gospel to their generation. They have come nearer to fulfilling their part of the Great Commission than any generation since. The sick were healed, the dead were raised, blind eyes were opened, evil spirits were cast out. The same works Christ had performed, they were now performing.

Jesus warned His disciples that in the last days false prophets would arise, and the love of many would wax cold. (See Matthew 24:12.) Paul wrote to Timothy to exhort him to remain faithful to his duties as a minister of the Gospel, warning him also that *"evil men and seducers shall wax worse and worse, deceiving, and being deceived"* (2 Timothy 3:13). John, the beloved disciple, described the state of the church before his passing, that some had already *"left their first love"* (Revelation 2:4); some had a name that they lived and were dead (Revelation 3:1); and some had allowed evil influences to defile their testimony (Revelation 2:14, 20). However, in each church of Revelation there were always a few who had *"not defiled their garments"* (Revelation 3:4). God has always had a remnant who were faithful, both in the church age and in Israel. The trunk of the tree was still there. There was still some life.

During the Middle Ages, the church fell into lethargy and apostasy. There was a great "falling away" from the original pattern of the early church. As the world came into the church, revival fires subsided. The tree was laid bare. Had Christ's death been in vain? Was this the way God had intended His church to go? No more than He intended the nation of Israel to fall away and bring reproach to the name of God.

God promised the church a spiritual restoration:

28 And it shall come to pass afterward, that I will pour out my spirit upon all flesh; and your sons and your daughters shall prophesy, your old men shall dream dreams, your young men shall see visions: 29 And also upon the servants and upon the handmaids in those days will I pour out my spirit.   *(Joel 2:28-29)*

God is raising up a mighty army of believers.

10 Who is she that looketh forth as the morning, fair as the moon, clear as the sun, and terrible as an army with banners?   *(Song of Solomon 6:10)*

God's church is going forth victorious, not defeated, led by her Captain of Salvation. The Lord spoke unto Peter, *"Thou art Peter, and upon this rock I will build my church; and the gates of hell shall not prevail against it"* (Matthew 16:18).

We rejoice in what happened in bygone days; how God moved in the early church and down through the ages, and even in the way God has moved and is moving in this generation. But we cannot live in the past. It is time to move on! Our young people would like to know what is for today. Like Gideon of old who had heard his forefathers tell of all the miracles of their day and how God delivered them from Egypt with a mighty hand, so our age wants to know, *"Where be all his miracles which our fathers told us of?"* (Judges 6:13).

We are not content just to hear about the miracles of the past. This generation would like to witness some personally. We are seeing some now. The days of miracles have not passed. We hear of miracles every day all over the world. God is healing those who are in the last stages of cancer, those troubled with heart disease, those whom doctors have given up on. Blind eyes and deaf ears are being opened. *"Jesus Christ the same yesterday, and today, and for ever"* (Hebrews 13:8).

Let me offer one word of warning: Do not restrict or limit the power of God, or the way He is moving or may move. The Lord rebuked Israel because they had *"limited the Holy One of Israel"* (Psalm 78:41). The Lord has never restricted Himself to any one method or church organization.

> *⁸For my thoughts are not your thoughts, neither are your ways my ways, saith the Lord.*
> *⁹For as the heavens are higher than the earth, so are my ways higher than your ways, and my thoughts than your thoughts.*   *(Isaiah 55:8-9)*

> *⁹But as it is written, Eye hath not seen, nor ear heard, neither have entered into the heart of man, the things which God hath prepared for them that love him.*
> *¹⁰But God hath revealed them unto us by his Spirit: for the Spirit searcheth all things, yea, the deep things of God.*
>   *(1 Corinthians 2:9-10)*

There is no limit to what we may have from God. We only limit ourselves.

> [22]*And Jesus answering saith unto them, have faith in God.*
> [23]*For verily I say unto you, that whosoever shall say unto this mountain, Be thou removed, and be thou cast into the sea: and shall not doubt in his heart, but shall believe that those things which he saith shall come to pass: he shall have whatsoever he saith.*
> [24]*Therefore I say unto you, What things soever ye desire, when ye pray, believe that ye receive them, and ye shall have them.*
> *(Mark 11:22-24)*

Whatever you say, that you shall have. There is power in words that are spoken in the name of Jesus. You create the words of your mouth. Speak faith, and you shall have what you say. Speak negatively—doubt, sickness, fear—and that is what you get. Speak life and you have life. We look with expectancy to an even greater move of the Holy Spirit as God's people move out in faith and accept the challenge that *"greater works than these shall he do; because I go unto my father"* (John 14:12). We will do the works of Christ.

It delights our heart to see the Gospel going out via the printed page, radio, television, and by satellite around the world. At this time, reports such as these are coming in from our missionaries and evangelists around the world: "Something wonderful is happening!" "Miracles of healing are taking place everywhere we go as God releases a new force of healing power." "I have never seen anything like it!" There is more to come.

> *[14]And this gospel of the kingdom shall be preached in all the world for a witness unto all nations; and then shall the end come.* (Matthew 24:14)

There is a stream of healing power flowing throughout the land. But many people will be like the children of Israel who had all the great promises of God for a land flowing with milk and honey, but could not enter in. *"So we see that they could not enter in because of unbelief"* (Hebrews 3:19). They limited the Holy One of Israel.

God provided a cloud by day and a pillar of fire by night. When it moved, they moved; when it stopped, they could go no farther. Let us determine in our hearts how God is moving and move with Him. Moses told the children of Israel, *"Ye have compassed this mountain long enough"* (Deuteronomy 2:3). It is time to go in and possess the land.

Jesus told His disciples: *"I must work the works of him that sent me, while it is day: the night cometh, when no man can work"* (John 9:4). The hour is growing late. The coming of the Lord is drawing near.

All signs indicate that there will be one generation when all things will be culminated. We believe it can't be much longer.

> *³²This generation shall not pass away, till all be fulfilled.*   *(Luke 21:32)*

> *²⁷For as the lightning cometh out of the east, and shineth even unto the west; so shall the coming of the Son of man be...*
> *⁴²Watch therefore; for ye know not what hour your Lord doth come.*
> *(Matthew 24:27, 42)*

He is not coming for a lukewarm, half-hearted church. He is building an army of faith people who are filled with the power of the Holy Ghost and who are totally committed to reach our generation for God. Let me remind you once again of Jesus' words:

> *¹²He that believeth on me, the works that I do shall he do also; and greater works than these shall he do; because I go to my father.*   *(John 14:12)*

No wonder He said, *"Ye shall receive power, after that the Holy Ghost is come upon you"* (Acts 1:8). What were the works of Christ? Opening of blind eyes, unstopping of deaf ears, causing the lame to walk, raising the dead, turning water into wine, stopping the storm, feeding the five thousand, and casting out demons.

"Now, Lord, do You really mean that we can do these things?" The disciples came up against a demon-possessed child. They were unable to cast the demon out. They were quite disturbed about it and asked Jesus, "Master, why can't we do this thing?" Jesus answered, "You can, by prayer and fasting." (See Matthew 17:19-21.)

We have limited the Holy One of Israel. Do not be surprised when you see the miracle-working power of God in action in our day, and more so as we see the day approaching. God will use every means possible to awaken the world to Christ.

This gospel of the kingdom must be preached in all the world as a witness before the Lord comes again.

During the last days, the church will be in travail, crying, *"Even so, come, Lord Jesus"* (Revelation 22:20). If we want Jesus to come back, we need to be doing all we can to bring Him back.

In the Old Testament we read where King David was in exile after the insurrection led by his son, Absalom. The people began to realize they were without a king and began to ask, *"Now therefore why speak ye not a word of bringing the kings back?"* (2 Samuel 19:10). David sent word to the elders saying, *"Why are ye the last to bring the king back?"* (v. 11). The king was waiting for an invitation to return. We must prepare the way for Christ's second coming even as John the Baptist prepared the way for His first coming.

You Ain't Seen Nothin' Yet!

[13]Looking for that blessed hope, and the glorious appearing of the great God and our Saviour Jesus Christ.   (Titus 2:13)

[20]He which testifieth these things saith, Surely I come quickly. Amen. Even so, come, Lord Jesus.   (Revelation 22:20)

About the Author

Clara Davis is an ordained minister of the Gospel. She and her husband, R. L., pastored and evangelized across the U.S. and overseas throughout their married life. Together they built six churches and raised three sons who are full-time ministers of the Gospel.

In 1972, R. L. Davis went home to be with the Lord. Clara has continued her service to God and is active in Women's Aglow. Drawing from her rich memories of God's outpouring of His power upon her family in the early 1900s, she still preaches revival and how to move on with the new move of God.